FLAMETHROWERS
OF THE GERMAN ARMY
1914-1945

Fred Koch

"Panzerkampfwagen III (Fl) Sd. Kfz. 141/3" used to train flamethrower troops. The commander of the vehicle was designated as the flame director, and the gunner as flame-shooter. The driver was simultaneously the flame-pumper. In all, 100 of the Flammpanzer III were produced from the end of 1942 to mid-1943. (WJS)

Schiffer Military History
Atglen, PA

BIBLIOGRAPHY

Military Intermediate Archives, Potsdam WF-02/6724; WF-03/31929; WF-10/2498; WF-10/13218; WF-10/13551; WF-10/13765
Army Directive 316: Engineer Service of All Weapons, Berlin 1941.
Army Directive 545: Service Manual for Large and Small Flamethrowers, Berlin 1937.
Army Directive 546: Small Flamethrower, Medium Flamethrower, Flamethrower Filler Wagon (Pf.21), Berlin 1941.
Army Directive 546/2: Flamethrower 41. Preliminary Description and Service Manual. Berlin 1942.
Army Directive 548: Flamethrower Protective Clothing, Equipment Description and Service Manual, Berlin 1940.
Army Directive 569: Engineer Handcart (Pf.22). Description and Service Manual.
Instruction Sheets 29/1-29/4: Engineer Service.
Cron, H., Die Organisation des deutschen Heeres im Weltkrieg, Berlin 1923.
Cron, H., Die Geschichte des deutschen Heeres 1914-1918, Berlin 1937.
Glahn, O., Pioniere einst und jetzt, Berlin 1936.
Reddemann, Die Totenkopf-Pioniere, Berlin 1937.
Spielberger, W. J., Militärfahrzeuge, Vol. 2-13, Stuttgart 1989-1992.
Periodicals: Signal, Die Wehrmacht, various illustrated newspapers, Völkischer Beobachter.
Waffenrevue.

Left: A flame-shooter of the German Army with the 1918-19 model "Small Flamethrower."

PHOTO CREDITS

Wolfgang Fleischer (WF), Werner Klotzsche (WK), Horst Scheibert (HS), Walter J. Spielberger (WJS), Gerhard Thiede (GT).

ACKNOWLEDGEMENTS

The author thanks Frau Anett, Frau S. Wetzig and Herren W. Fleischer, Chr. Hermann, G. Herr, H.-J. Janaczeck, N. Lasse, H. Scheibert, W.J. Spielberger and G. Thiede for their generous assistance and for making photographic material available.

Translated from the German by Edward Force.

Printed in China.
ISBN: 0-7643-0264-7

This book was originally published under the title,
Flammenwerfer des deutschen Heeres,
by Podzun-Pallas Verlag.

We are interested in hearing from authors with book ideas on related topics.

Published by Schiffer Publishing Ltd.
77 Lower Valley Road
Atglen, PA 19310
Phone: (610) 593-1777
FAX: (610) 593-2002
E-mail: Schifferbk@aol.com.
Please write for a free catalog.
This book may be purchased from the publisher.
Please include $2.95 postage.
Try your bookstore first.

FOREWORD

Since ancient times, fire has fascinated and terrified mankind. Without making this medium useful, no progress could have been made. With no other element of nature are the proverbial words "light and shadow" so closely related. Along with the provision of heat, it embodies great powers of destruction. Making use of heat and power militarily was limited only by the technical means of making it mobile. After appropriate ways were found, a new type of weapon appeared in the German Army literally overnight. In a few weeks, a "handful of people" had become a unit of more than 3000 men. At the same speed at which it arise and expanded, it shrank again, though, and in the end it never amounted to more than independent troops. The main reason for this was that flamethrowers could be used only tactically, and their reasons for use were limited to shock-troop operations and local defense.

Until now, the history of the flamethrower units and their equipment has only been touched upon slightly. With this volume, an appropriate overview shall be created for the first time. But since the sources of information, now as before, are very limited, with information and data scattered, even after years of study there are still gaps. Although sufficient photographic material could be gathered, there are places where pictures that left something to be desired had to be used. The author hereby asks for understanding and is open to any helpful criticism.

GERMAN FLAMETHROWERS 1914-1945

In the very first years of the war that was later called "World War I", the German military planning went to pieces. The 'Schliefen Plan" did not work. In the beginning, a considerable part of Western Europe could be occupied by disregarding the neutrality of Belgium, but the offensives of the Central Powers (Germany, Austria-Hungary, Italy, Turkey and Bulgaria) against the Entente (France, Great Britain, Russia and Japan) came to a stop on the Marne in September 1914, after only 45 days.

The battle of the Marne was the first and likewise the decisive turning point of this war. After the fronts between the Aisne and the Vosges stopped moving, both sides tried flanking operations in the north in the so-called "race to the sea" (September to November 1914). But the German Army did not succeed in reaching the French Channel ports. On the other hand, all of Belgium was occupied.

After the failure of the Flanders offensive at Ypres, the front from the North Sea to the Swiss border ceased to move as of November 1914. Further attempts to bring the front back into motion had only local success. A positional war, characterized by great expenditure of material, dominated the times that followed. Feverishly, both sides began to seek new expedients or turn back to old ones in order to overcome the lack of movement. The German Army High Command (O.H.L.) had ever-greater hopes for the use of flamethrowers, along with poison gases, large-caliber guns, hand grenades, machine weapons and many others.

A shock troop with "large flamethrowers" is ready to attack. At least three men were needed to operate the device, one to direct the nozzle, a second to carry the hose, which could be up to 30 meters long, and a third to activate the valves of the fuel tank.

THE FIREMEN

The idea of using liquid fire as a weapon of war was not born in the twentieth century. It is reported from ancient times that in 424 B.C. the Greeks, during the siege of the city of Deleon in the Peloponnesian War, used "Greek fire", a device similar to a flamethrower. With the help of a powerful stream of air, a mixture of pitch, sulphur, saltpeter, oil and burned chalk was blown through an iron pipe. Since these flame pipes were very heavy to handle and were only effective in close contact with the enemy, they were soon forgotten again.

Three 100-liter tanks of burning oil, with the bottles of nitrogen used with them, are connected to each other in order to lengthen the jet of flame.

With the development of artillery and handguns toward the end of the fifteenth century, the use of liquid fire seemed to be outmoded once and for all. Such weapons have a large range, with great destructive power and little range of dispersion, can be used more simply and quickly, and are less dependent on wind and weather. Only in the Russo-Japanese War of 1905 were burning liquids once again used for purposes of attack and defense.

In Germany as well, several years before World War I, so-called "fire pipes" were utilized to smoke out the crews of defensive trenches in fortifications and the like. They represented one of the simplest types of flamethrowers. The Berlin engineer Fiedler had carried on the first experiments with them and built appropriate apparatus. Independently of Fiedler's work, the director of the Landwehr Engineer Company, Reddemann, during a drill of warfare against fortifications at Posen in 1907, had used "flamethrowers", with the help of the Posen professional firemen subordinated to him, to defend a portion of the fortifications. The flamethrowers were simulated by jets of water from a steam sprayer. The idea of spraying liquid fire continued to interest Reddemann after that drill. Now he began to develop apparatus designed for that principle of action.

An attack with "large flamethrowers" on the western front near Lens in September 1917.

THE FUNCTIONING

A flamethrower attack. The flame tube usually had to be held by two men.

The work of Reddemann showed that sprays of flame could be created and put into use tactically with relatively little effort. The technical functioning principle can be described as follows: Into a container with an easily flammable oil mixture, nitrogen is injected under high pressure and sprayed to a distance of several meters. As the spray of oil is ejected from the pipe, the oil is ignited and kept burning by a glowing ignition device. To attain a strong effect on morale, an oil mixture was used that produced clouds of black smoke as it burned. In places where there was a danger of being recognized by enemy artillery, an oil mixture that produced only a thin, barely visible bit of smoke was used.

Without waiting for agreement from the military leadership, Reddemann began in 1912-13, with the support of several enthusiasts, to prepare models for two sizes of flamethrowing apparatus in the workshop of the Posen Fire Department.

A shock troop with the first-type flamethrower makes its way through trenches on the western front to approach the enemy.

The "Large Flamethrower" was to be used chiefly in trench warfare, in cut-through country and in the defense of municipalities. It had a high weight, was hard to move, and could only be operated standing or lying. The tank of the flamethrower had a capacity of 100 liters of burning oil, which could be sprayed 45 meters for three-quarters of a minute at a pressure of 15 atmospheres. As a rule, several tanks were to be connected together in order to achieve a longer period of effectiveness. The resulting combustion gases from the plumes of flame, with an appropriate wind direction, could attain a range of up to 100 meters. In order to expand the effective range even more for offensive actions, various forms of attack were selected in the war, for example, the advance of the pipe holder with a hose up to 30 meters long, or the construction of long tunnels between one's own position and that of the enemy.

The "Small Flamethrower" was to be carried on the back of one man. The first design, though, had such a heavy weight that off-road movement required an immense expenditure of energy. It was replaced very soon by a smaller apparatus, the weight of which more or less equaled that of a marching pack. This allowed the carrier to move in short bursts across the terrain, throw himself into cover, and cover long stretches with and ahead of the enemy. The small portable flamethrower carried about ten liters of burning oil. With an effective duration of 15 seconds, it attained a range of 20 meters.

The original version of the "Small Flamethrower" had the shape of a tank, with the nitrogen container attached to either the side or the back. This picture shows clearly that this device must have been too heavy for shock troops. The flame-shooter bears the symbol of the flame troops, the "death's-head", on his sleeve. (WF)

Demonstration of the "Small Flamethrower" at a training camp. (WF)

German infantrymen with flamethrowers and hand grenades storming the heights of the "Dead Man" on March 15, 1916. The flame-shooter in the background carries the long tank on his back, and it can be seen clearly that the nitrogen container is attached to the back of it. Climbing a slope while carrying this weight required all one's strength.

Under the protection of clouds of flamethrower smoke, the troops leave their trenches on the Somme and move out to attack. These troops are also equipped with the earlier version. Since only the tank can be seen, the nitrogen container must be attached on the side.

IMPORTANCE

When the first special unit was set up on January 18, 1915, under the name of "Flamethrower Unit Reddemann", it consisted of only 48 engineers, the majority of whom were former firemen.

At first the High Army Command was very doubtful about this "new" weapon. But right after its first action on February 26, 1915, during the attack on Malaucourt, the establishment of a "flamethrower company" by April of 1915 was ordered.

After the establishment of additional units, the "III. Guard Engineer Battalion" was formed, and in April 1916 all the flamethrower units were brought together in the "Guard Reserve Engineer Regiment." Until the war ended, this regiment consisted of three battalions and twelve combat companies, one field testing company, and one field training company, over 3000 men in all.

The flamethrower companies were made up of three marching platoons of five squad each, one machine-gun and one replacement squad. Each squad had two flamethrowers. The machine-gun squads had two light machine guns and one light mine launcher each. The regiment was called on for no other engineer services than flamethrower action.

Every company had thirty to forty "small flamethrowers" and the necessary reserves of materials and fuels. In addition, they carried twelve to fifteen "large flamethrowers" and reserve materials with them on trucks.

The field testing company constantly carried out tests to improve the flamethrowing apparatus, had the tasks of repairing damaged flamethrowers and regulating supplies of oil, igniters, nitrogen and the like. During the course of the war, they set up a "flamethrower factory", located with their regimental staff in France. This had to be moved several times during the war. Its production had to meet all the army's requirements in flamethrowers and supplies.

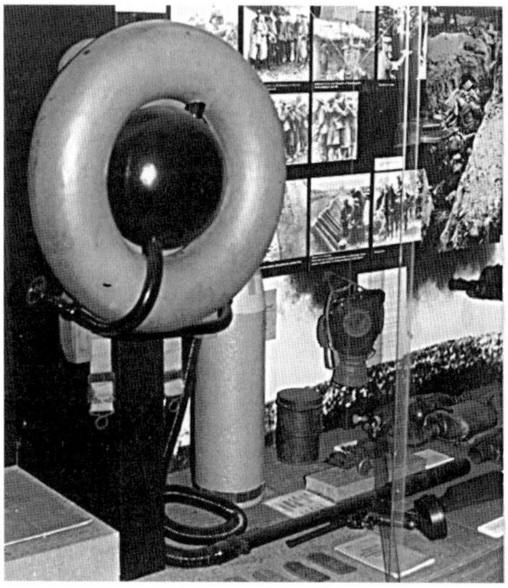

A view of the "flamethrower factory" on the western front. It had to be moved often. Abandoned blacksmith shops offered the best facilities for new quarters.

The final form of the portable flamethrower. It was clearly smaller. The outer ring contained the burning oil, with the hemispherical container for the nitrogen in the middle. This restored "Kl.Fm.W." is in the display of the MHM in Dresden.(GT)

The supply train of the "Guard Reserve Engineer Regiment" consisted of horsedrawn wagons. To be easily mobile and bring the equipment as close to the front as possible, only "light field wagons" could be considered. This is a one-horse wagon with spare nitrogen containers and tubes for the "large flamethrower."

EFFECTIVENESS

The use of the flamethrower showed tactical effects in three ways. Along with the physical effect of the flames on the enemy and his weapons or equipment, the enemy was also influenced psychologically. As soon as he learned of the planned use of flamethrowers, the enemy often withdrew so as not to be within their range. Thus favorable prerequisites for an infantry attack were created.

About the effect of flamethrowers at Fort Vaux, a German officer, obviously still affected by his impressions of this action, wrote in a letter of June 3, 1916: "It was 9:30 AM. The fiery catastrophe broke in on the French. A roaring sea of fire rolled onto them. The enemy saw glowing, flickering tongues of flame coming at him out of huge clouds of smoke, but saw no men and no equipment. Like a natural event of powerful force, the appearance depressed him. . ."

In a report of the 45th Reserve Division to the Army High Command in August 1918, it was said: "In the further course of action, the flamethrower took part very effectively in the elimination of machine-gun nests. Where there was no support from flamethrowers, the conquest of the machine-gun nests with hand grenades usually took a much longer time and cost us more losses. Wherever they got into action, the flamethrowers successfully supported the attack. Beyond that, their activity made a very favorable impression on the morale of our infantry."

Although the action of the flamethrower helped to create more favorable conditions for attack, they always brought about only local success.

A "Small Flamethrower" assault.

It was not so much the destructive power of the flames as the psychological effect of the sea of flame and the "black wall" of smoke that drove the enemy out of his positions and thus created favorable conditions for infantry action — as long as the wind did not change.

While only fifteen flame fights took place during 1915, their numbers increased to 160 in 1916, to 165 the next year, and in 1918 to 296, with one almost every day.

All in all, the individual parts of the "Guard Reserve Engineer Regiment" carried out 653 flamethrower attacks, of which 535 gained success (82%) while 118 were without useful results (18%).

A basic change in positional warfare, though, could not be achieved through the use of flamethrowers. The fact that the Entente highly regarded the effect of the German flamethrower units is shown by, among other things, Article 171 of the peace treaty of Versailles, which banned the possession, manufacture and importing of flamethrowers.

Nevertheless, the development of the flamethrower never stopped, despite the terms of the Versailles treaty. For reasons of secrecy, the developmental work and tests were carried out for the most part by associated firms in other countries.

A large-scale attack with flamethrowers near Rheims in 1917. A huge wall of fire and smoke rolled toward the enemy, utilizing the wind.

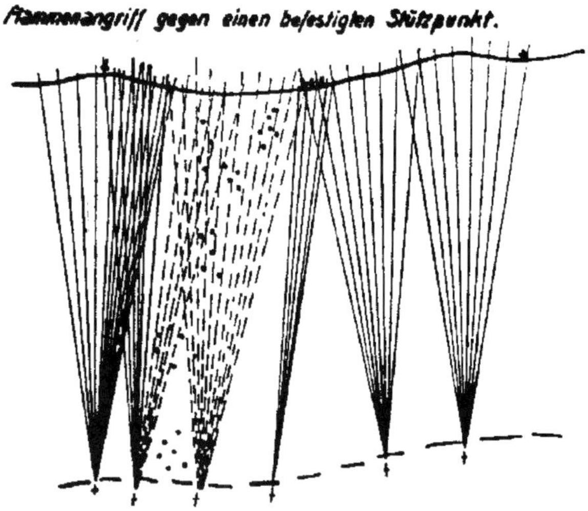

Flame attack against a fortified support point.

Fortified position of the enemy

Our own attack front

Advancing flame and shock troop

Fortified enemy support point

Effective fire of our machines and guns

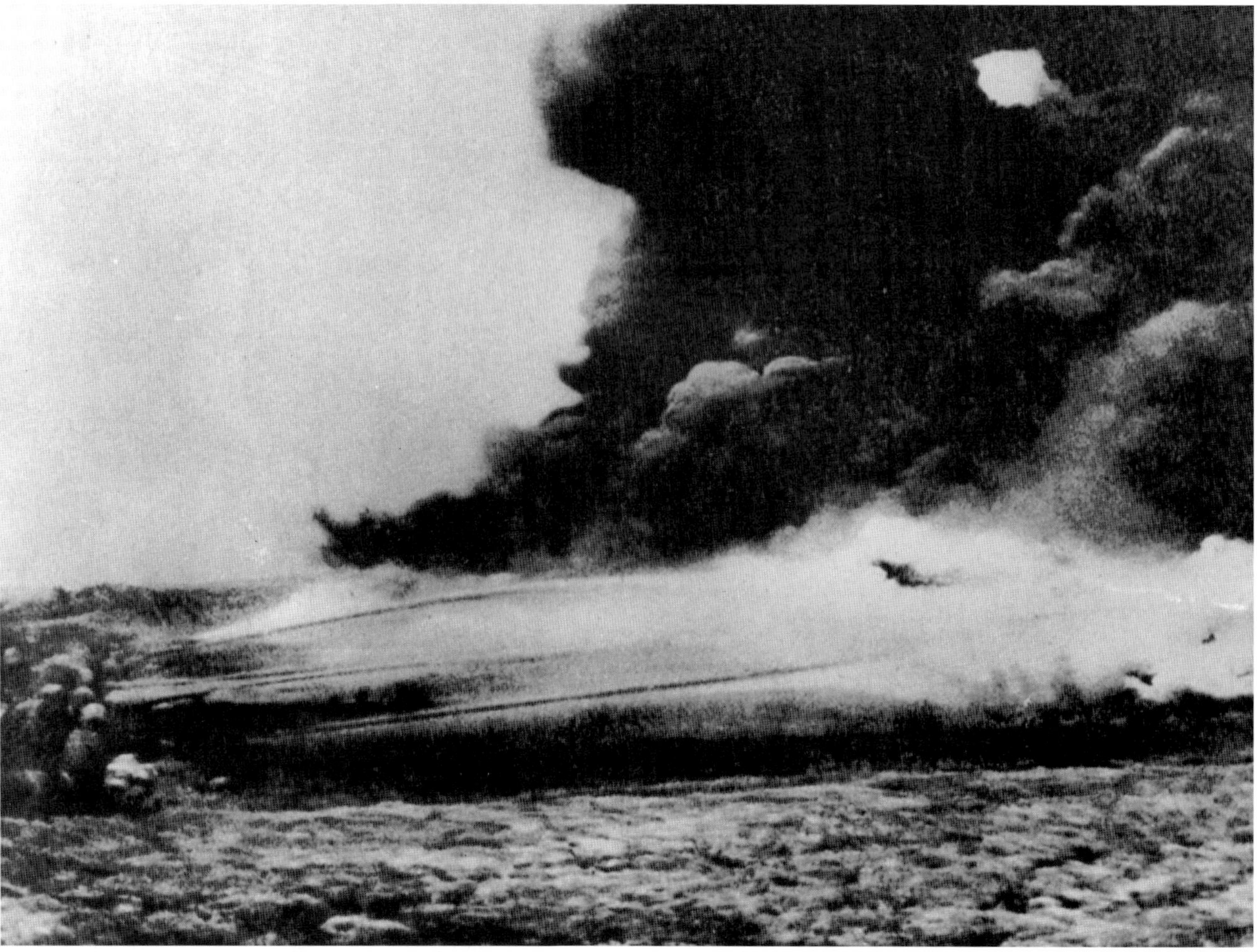

A flamethrower attack on the entire front sector near Lens in September 1917. In the lee of the tongues of flame and clouds of smoke, the infantry moved ahead and drove the enemy out of the foremost trenches.

A training camp near Charleroi on October 1918. Members of a flamethrower squad practice the use of their weapons against armored vehicles. The enemy tanks were represented by two A7V assault tanks (above) and one captured "Mark IV" tank (below).

A complete flamethrower squad marches through the streets of Berlin during the armed uprisings at the end of 1918.

FLAMETHROWERS OF THE WEHRMACHT

For the German Wehrmacht, its leadership foresaw three types of flamethrowers. They were described as small portable, medium driveable, and large fixed. The last were intended for installation in fortifications and, at a later point in time, in armored vehicles.

The central direction of the development was taken over by the Weapon Proving Ground 5/1 (Engineers) of the Army Testing Station at Kummersdorf. After the work on flamethrowers and testing of them had been concluded for the time being, the Army High Command (O.K.H.), through the Reich Minister of Aviation and Commander of the Luftwaffe Hermann Göring, as the man in charge of the four-year plan, awarded the first contracts for series production of flamethrowers, on July 11, 1938, to the following armament manufacturers: The Karlsruhe and Lübeck works of the Deutsche Waffen- und Munitionsfabriken A.G. (D.W.M.) were to manufacture portable and driveable flamethrowers. Later the firm of Hagenuk in Kiel would also be drawn into production. The contract for the production of carrying racks went to the Stiegelmeier firm in Herfort, Westphalia. The first production contract included 168 portable, thirty of them as instructional devices for the Weapon Proving Ground 5, and 35 driveable flamethrowers. The instructional devices were to be delivered by the end of June 1938, those for the troops by September 1938. In all, by the end of 1938, 1000 devices were to be produced. The firms of "Minimax" in Neuruppin, Hagenuk in Kiel, and the D.W.M. works in Karlsruhe and Lübeck were given contracts to produce the fixed flamethrowers. At a later point in time, the firm of Wegelin & Hübener in Halle was to take over part of the production. By March 31, 1939 154 devices were to be produced, along with 230 each of tanks and containers.

In the years from 1934 to 1938, the D.W.M., in close cooperation with the Engineer Inspection at the Army Proving Ground in Kummersdorf, developed the "Small Flamethrower." For reasons of production technology, they returned to a cylindrical design. Although the use of steel alloys allowed the walls to be considerably thinner, and the more highly compressed nitrogen could also be stored in a small compressed-gas bottle, the gross weight was still about 36 kilograms.

Flamethrower training in the 4th Platoon, 4th Company, Panzer Engineer Battalion 13 of the 14th Panzer Division in the spring of 1939. The newly enlisted soldiers are taught to operate the "Small Flamethrower" and use their first bursts of flame in various forms of attack. In training, a light burning oil was used, which rose in burning and left only the plume of flame and the smoke gases. This was achieved by blending light tar oils and petroleum.*

LIGHT PORTABLE FLAMETHROWER

The first "canister flamethrower" that the testing departments of the Wehrmacht released for troop testing, and that was introduced in the engineer units in mid-1938, was the "Small Flamethrower" (often referred to in post-1945 publications as the "Flammenwerfer 34 bez. 35"). The cylindrical metal pressure tank was filled with 11.8 liters of a blend of light and heavy tar oils (Burning Oil No. 19). In many cases, benzol thickened with motor oil or petroleum was used. The smaller bottle on the left side, serving to propel the mixture, was filled with five liters of compressed nitrogen. With a filling pressure of 25 atmospheres, the range of the plume of flame was about 25 meters. The device could sustain fire for a maximum of ten seconds. At the mouth of the tube, the mixture was ignited by a glow-ignition mechanism. The very first troop tests showed that the "Small Flamethrower", with its gross weight of 36 kilograms, was too heavy. The engineer troops thus requested that the development of a lighter version be expedited.

A shock troop attacks, supported by a "Panzerkampfwagen I Ausf. B Sd.Kfz. 101." The flameshooter runs ahead of the wall of smoke.

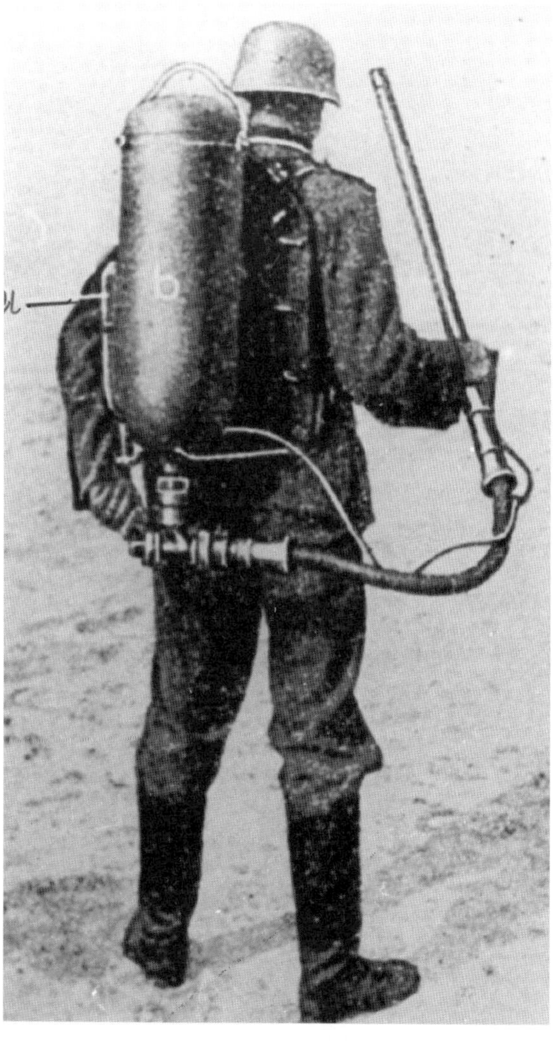

Left:
a = Compressed nitrogen container (5 liters)
b = Burning oil container (11.8 liters)

To transport the flamethrowers, tubes, igniters, explosives, etc., to the foremost areas, the Engineer Handcart Pf. 22 (Pionierfahrzeug 22) was used. It was made with either pneumatic tires or all-steel wheels. It had an empty weight of 885 kilograms and could carry loads up to 300 kg.

The use of the flamethrower was only effective when it moved fast and surprised the enemy. Since the range of the plumes of flame was between 20 and 25 meters, it was necessary to move as close to the enemy lines as inconspicuously as possible and cross open areas in as short a time as possible.

A shock troop with the "Small Flamethrower" during the training of flamethrower troops in the spring of 1940. (WF)

A shock troop with the "Small Flamethrower" during the training of flamethrower troops in the spring of 1940. (WF)

Above and right: A flamethrower attack on a French fortification ahead of the Maginot Line in May 1940.

Engineers, equipped with the "Small Flamethrower", attack French fortifications in the Maginot Line.

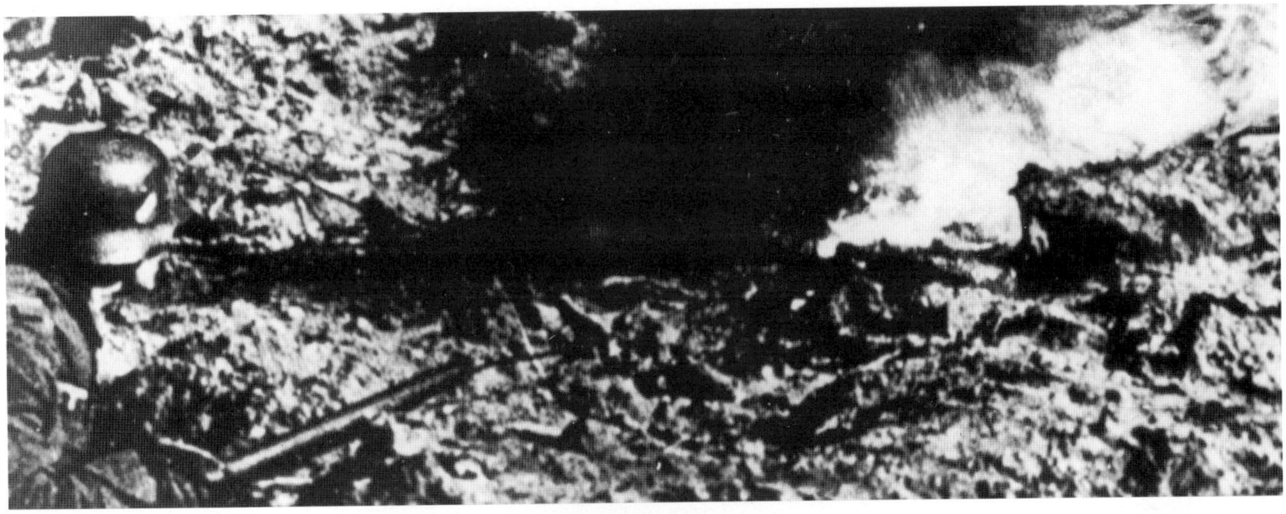

Under the protection of clouds of flamethrower smoke, the troops leave their trenches on the Somme and move out to attack. These troops are also equipped with the earlier version. Since only the tank can be seen, the nitrogen container must be attached on the side.

An engineer troop of the 7th Panzer Division crosses a blown-up bridge over the Meuse. Below: Use of the "Kl. Fm. W." against a machine-gun position in the Balkans in 1941.

Another picture of flamethrower training, as a soldier practices attacking an enemy system of positions with the "Small Flamethrower."

Left: Russia, September-October 1941. A shock troop with "Small Flamethrower", :Machine Gun 34" and "Machine Pistol 38/40", strengthened with an "Assault Gun III Type E, Sd.Kfz. 142" (platoon leader's or battery combat vehicle) during the combat for the harbor area of Novorosiysk.

Right: Flamethrower action on the Russian steppes in the autumn of 1942.

Below: Flamethrowers used in building combat in the winter.

Since there was at first no better suggestion from the industry, Weapon Proving Ground 5/1 continued the development of a portable flamethrower, based on the type that was used in World War I. The weight of this flamethrower could, it was true, be reduced to 21.3 liters by limiting the burning oil to 7.5 liters, but the Army Testing Department rejected it because of technical shortcomings. The smallest splinters or contact with fixed objects often caused it to crack. This shock-troop weapon, referred to today as "Flamethrower small, improved" or Flamethrower 40", only reached the troops in small numbers. In order to reduce the weight of the flamethrower to 18 kilograms, make it handier and reduce its surface, its successor, officially designated "Flamethrower 41", was fitted with two relatively small cylindrical pressure tanks, one above the other. The lower one was larger and held 7.5 liters of burning oil, while the smaller upper one held three liters of compressed hydrogen. The range of the flame was between 30 and 35 meters. But since there were frequent failures of the igniting apparatus, especially in low outdoor temperatures, a new tube for this flamethrower was introduced for troop use as of the spring of 1942. Ignition was done via spray cartridges. Every flamethrower included a magazine of ten ignition cartridges.

Two of the improved "Small Flamethrower" that were introduced by the Army Weapons Office in mid-1940. The right one seems to be an almost exact copy of the "Kl. Fm. W." of World War I. It differs from its predecessor, though, in its nozzle tube and the smaller container of compressed gas.

In the Fm. W. at left, the two ring-shaped containers are made of folded metal, similar to the "folded cartridges." The total weights of these devices could be reduced considerably, but they offered a larger surface for the enemy to aim at.

Only rarely was the improved version of the "Small Flamethrower" used by the troops. This soldier on the Russian steppes, equipped with the "Kl. Fm. W.", belonged to the Panzergrenadier Division "Grossdeutschland." As a personal weapon, every flamethrower man carried a pistol. (HS)

Above and below: The first flamethrower that was officially designated with its year of introduction was the "Fm. W. 41." It finally met the requirements of the troops and, with 70,000 of them built, was the most often-built flamethrower of World War II. The "Fm. W. 41" shown in the picture above belongs to the Military History Museum in Dresden. (GT)

When the army was reorganized in 1935, seven engineer battalions were planned. At the beginning of 1939, the number was raised to 65 battalions, and as of September 1, 1939, 128 had been established. Every engineer battalion had the fourth platoon of its fourth company as a flamethrower platoon, to which nine flamethrowers belonged. Such a platoon consisted of one officer, five non-commissioned officers and twelve flame-shooters.

Along with the engineer battalions of the divisions, the army engineers and special units also received the "Fm. W. 41." In addition, at least one of these flamethrowers was among the equipment of every armored railroad train.

Although flamethrowers were originally regarded as shock-troop weapons, they took on ever-greater importance to Germany's military leadership as defensive weapons during the course of World War II. As early as 1942, the German armament industry produced 4618 of the "Flamethrowers 41", with production rising to 11,480 in 1943 and 44,280 in 1944. As of March 1944, monthly production totaled 4000 units. In spite of that, losses at the fronts could scarcely be replaced. Along with the Wehrmacht, the Luftwaffe received 1070 "Fm. W. 41", the Navy 837 units, the police 89, and 1310 of these flamethrowers were turned over to Germany's allies. On March 1, 1945 there were still 694 "Flamethrower 41" in the arsenals.

Attempts to improve the "Fm. W. 41", though, never brought the desired results. The "Flamethrower 43", with its total weight of 24 kilograms and capacity of nine liters of burning oil, was regarded as too heavy, and the "Flamethrower 44", with a weight of 4.4 kg and capacity of four liters of oil, was seen as insufficient.

Under contract to the German paratroops, the Borsigwalde works of the D.W.M. began in October 1944 to build the "Attack Flamethrower 46." After the formation of the "German Volkssturm" had been ordered on September 26, 1944, the Volkssturm was also to be supplied, as of the end of 1944, with this device, then known as "People's Flamethrower 46" or "Defensive Flamethrower 46." This light and easily produced weapon consisted of a long cylindrical pressure container (fighting weight 3.6 kg, empty weight 2.64 kg, dimensions 600 x 75 x 190 mm) with two rings for a carrying belt, a handle with trigger, a 9 mm nozzle and a holder for the propellant cartridge. The plume of flame lasted half a second and reached 30 to 40 meters. In October 1944, 1000 of these "wonder weapons" were produced, in November 1944 the production was increased to 3500, and in December 1944 to 7000. On March 1, 1945 there were still 3580 "Abw. Fm. W. 46" in the Wehrmacht's arsenals.

In mid-1944, the Waffen-SS, independently of the Army, also had a light flamethrower developed. It weighed only 2.8 kilograms in all. But it was never introduced. There was also a multiple-fire flamethrower developed by the Waffen-SS. It had a total weight of 14 kg, and its burning oil was to be ignited by powder tablets. When the war ended, there were also projects in hand at the D.W.M. in Berlin-Borsigwalde and at "Minimax" in Neuruppin for a "Small Fortress Flamethrower", which was supposed to be used for short-range defense in armored turret positions and machine-gun installations. Its range was 20 meters.

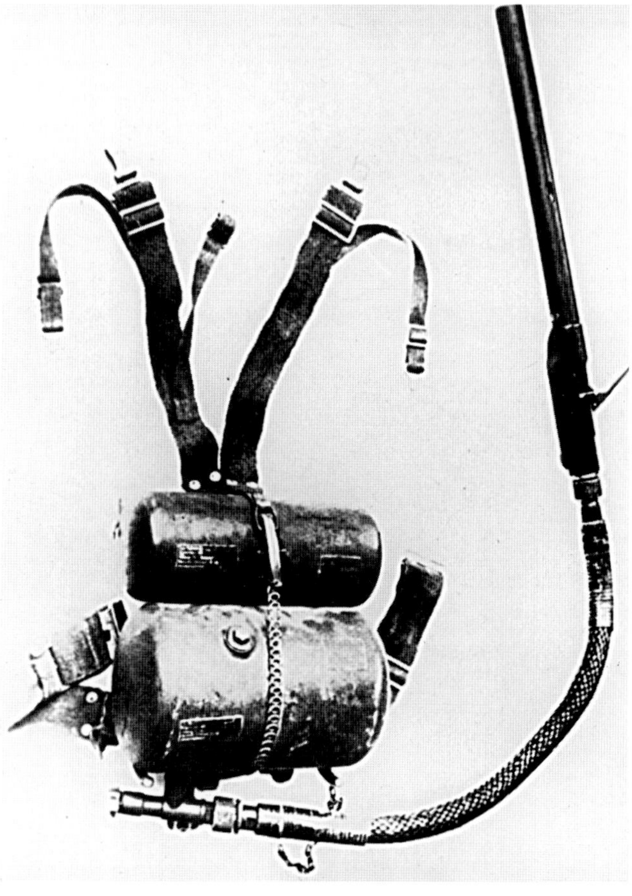

Above: Two flamethrower men with their weapons in street combat. In the background is an "Assault Gun IV." (WF)

Below: A paratrooper with "Fm. W. 41" in a flame attack.

A shock troop of paratroopers attacks a Russian village in the winter of 1943.

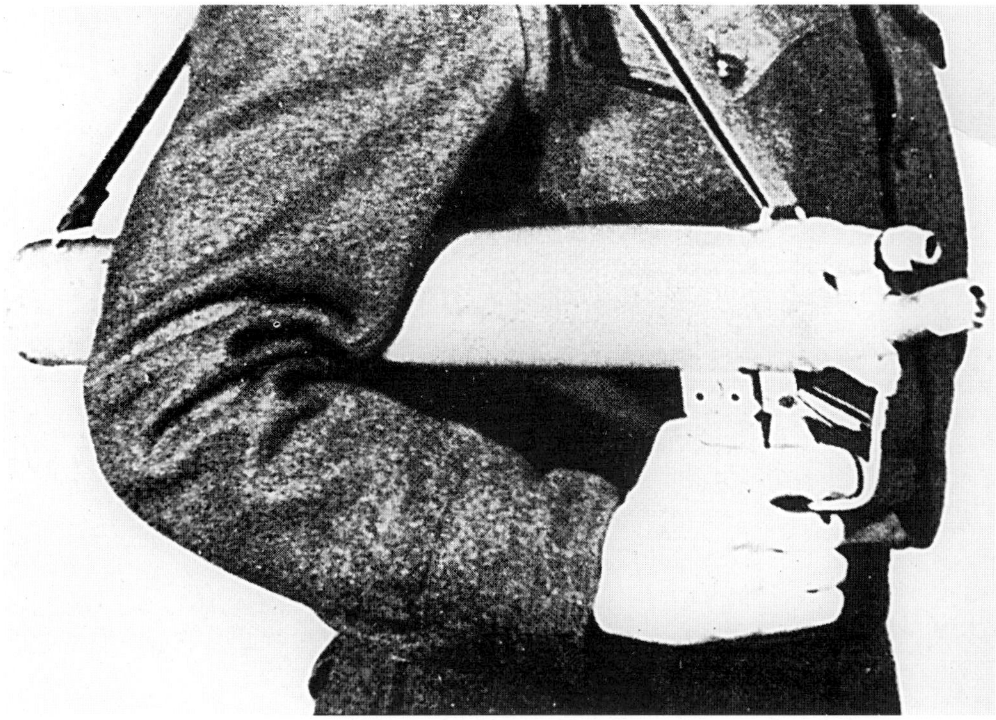

The way to carry the "Attack Fm. W. 46" is demonstrated by a British soldier after the war. After the weapon was supplied almost exclusively to the "German Volkssturm" as of the end of 1944, its designation to "Defensive Fm. W. 46." The arsenals listed it as "People's Flamethrower 46."

Likewise from the Dresden Museum is this "Defensive Flamethrower 46." The picture clearly shows the extremely simple construction of this device. (GT)

MEDIUM DRIVEABLE FLAMETHROWERS

The "Canister Flamethrower" contained only a small supply of burning oil. Thus its firepower was very limited. To have a large supply no hand, the German weapons industry built, as of 1935, the "Medium Flamethrower" on a wheeled chassis. The gross weight was 102 kilograms, and the pressure container held thirty liters of burning oil. The complete time of fire was some 25 seconds, and the range was between 25 and 32 meters. With this device, up to fifty bursts of fire could be given. In this weapon, the burning oil and nitrogen container was attached to a small rubber-tired handcart, which was pulled by two flamethrower men. A special "Flamethrower Trailer" built for halftrack towing tractors attained a range of 40 to 50 meters with a firing time of up to 24 seconds. Both models, though, proved to be too unhandy, and were rejected by the troops. They were used only by the engineer units in the western campaigns, after which they were, if still useful for combat, turned over to the Army equipment offices.

Above and below: The tank of the "Medium Flamethrower" was transported on a pneumatic-tired handcart.

Left: The "Flamethrower Trailer" was meant to be towed by the "Light Towing Tractor 3 t H kl 6, Sd.Kfz. 11." The towing vehicle had a special body for servicing and repairing all the flamethrowers used by the troops.

Above: Flamethrower men of Panzer Engineer Battalion 13 of the 14th Panzer Division during a pause in training for "handling the Medium Flamethrower."

Below: A flamethrower squad, completely equipped, waits for the command to take action.

COPIED - THE DEFENSIVE FLAMETHROWER 42

When the German Wehrmacht attacked the Red Army in the summer of 1941, a broad spray of flame suddenly and unexpectedly shout out of the ground at the German soldiers in several combat sectors. When they searched the terrain, the German engineers found the dug-in Russian FOG-1 flamethrowers. These fixed-position flamethrowers became the most often-built type made by the Russian war industry during the course of World War II. From 1941 to 1945, 15,000 of these devices were built in all. The German military leadership was so impressed by the effect of these weapons that they immediately decided to have the devices copied or have those they found made reusable. Under the designation "Defensive Flamethrower 42", 50,000 of them were contracted for, and all were delivered by June 1944. By the end of 1942 there were already 19,890 of them in the hands of the Engineer units. In 1943, 27,869 of them were built, and in 1944 the last 4162 were made.

Because of the improving situation of the Red Army on the German-Russian front, the need for means of barrage had suddenly increased. The "Abw. Fm. W. 42" substantially met the requirements of the Wehrmacht leadership. With the use of several flamethrowers, an area up to 150 meters wide could be closed off. The time of effect, though, was limited to three seconds.

The main pieces of the device were the burning-oil container (empty weight 32.5 kg), tube with nozzle, seal disc, pressure cartridge and igniter. The total weight of the filled device was about 65 kg. As igniters for the pressure cartridge and the burning oil, two identical electrical igniters were used. Thus each device required two of them. These were replaced by the Glow Ignition Device 37 or 39. To fill the flamethrower, 30 liters of burning oil were used. The device, though, could also be used with a smaller amount of oil, as long as it was not less than 20 liters. With each "Abw. Fm. W. 42" were ten pressure cartridges, twenty igniters and ten explosive plates.

Russian flamethrowers that were dug up by German engineers. All the usable devices were equipped with German pressure cartridges, igniters and seal discs and reused.

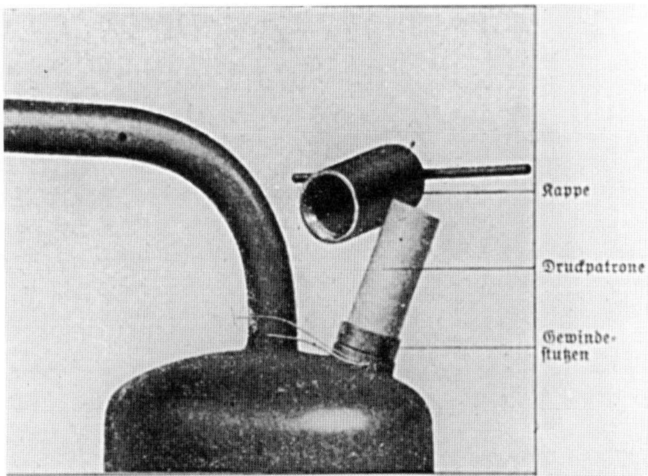

As long as the "Defensive Flamethrower 42" was not destroyed or mechanically damaged on the battlefield, it could be refilled at any time. Then the seal disc and the pressure cartridge were also replaced, and the device was ready for use again.

Below: An "Abw. Fm. W. 42" has its glow igniter device attached by a German engineer and is then ready to be buried. (WF)

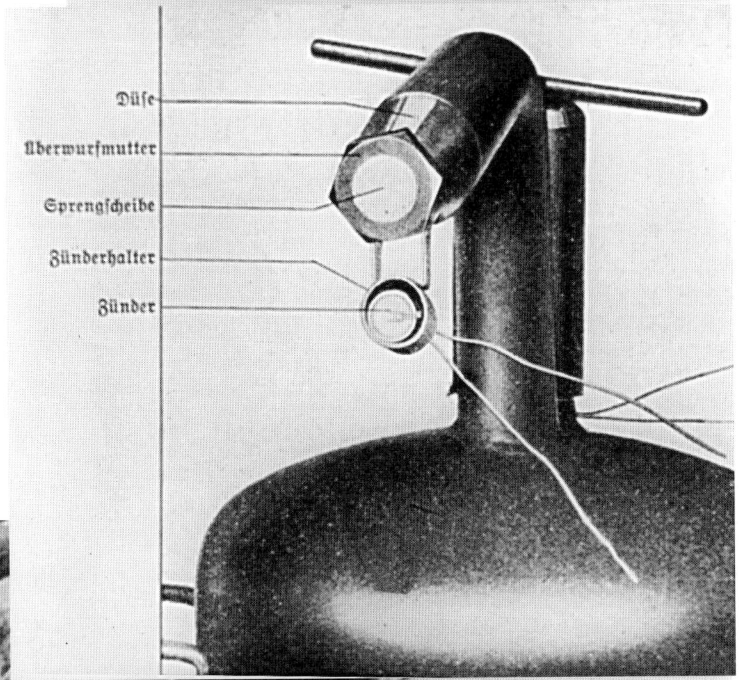

FLAMETHROWERS ON ARMORED VEHICLES

In order to use flamethrowers for defense, the German armament industry produced the so-called "fixed" devices. Their variety became more and more diverse as the war went on, but their production never reached large numbers, although the Army continually made advances in this direction. The production of armored vehicles with flamethrowers always had to be secondary to the production of tanks with armor-piercing weapons. The first "Panzer I (Fl)" was developed from the "Light Battle Tank I, Sd.Kfz. 101." This was presumably rebuilt in the workshops of the German Afrikakorps, for the use of only one of these vehicles, in Tunisia in 1941, is known to date. The "Flammpanzer I" (no official designation) is said to have been fitted, in place of the righthand machine gun in the turret, with a "Small Flamethrower" from the developmental year of 1934-35. The lefthand machine gun was not removed. The burning-oil container and the compressed-gas tank were attached inside the fighting compartment. On January 21, 1939 the Weapon Proving Ground 6, in accordance with WaPrüf 5, awarded a contract for the development of the first production "Flammpanzer." The Maschinenfabrik Augsburg-Nürnberg firm was accordingly to rebuild the armored hull of the "Light Battle Tank II Types D and E, Sd.Kfz. 121 (Type 8/LaS 138)" made by Daimler-Benz in Berlin-Marienfelde, and the Waggonfabrik Wegmann & Co. AG in

The "Panzer I" with "Small Flamethrower" installed by the Afrikakorps in Tunisia in 1941. Although there was talk of several such vehicles, this cannot be confirmed to date. It cane be presumed that there was only one such vehicle, which was only used by the troops for a short time. Its utility in desert warfare was questionable. The effect of the flamethrower is based mainly on its high destructive power in the nearby area. In areas like North Africa, in which one's view extended to the horizon, the maximum direct shot ranges of all flat-trajectory guns could be utilized, and the vehicle could have been destroyed at long range by armor-piercing weapons.

"Panzerkampfwagen II D (Fl), Sd.Kfz. 122" used by Panzer Unit 100 (Fl) in Russia. The unit can be determined by the rings painted on the back of the turret.

Kassel-Rothenditmold was to provide the appropriate components. The choice of the D/E version of the Panzer II was surely made for reasons of the greater space available in that vehicle. With a new front body design and the direct attachment of the Variorex gearbox to the Maybach engine (only the crankshaft with divider drive was located in front), more room was created beside the driver.

This space could now be used for the flamethrower operator. The new body, instead of the turret with 2 cm K. 38 L/55 tank gun and machine gun, had a smaller one armed only with MG 34. On each of the front track covers there was now a small turning turret, in which the two flamethrowers were housed. Their field of traverse was 180 degrees. The burning-oil containers were mounted outside the body on either side, in armored boxes attached to the hull. The range of the plume of flame was about 35 meters. Eighty bursts of fire, each 2 to 3 seconds long, could be fired.

The production of these vehicles, known as "Panzerkampfwagen II (Fl) Sd.Kfz. 122", began in the spring of 1939. On September 1, 1939 the newly established 1st Flammpanzer Unit received the first three vehicles. On April 1, 1940 four more arrived. By June 19, 1940 the number of "Flammpanzer II" in use by the troops had increased to sixteen. By October 1940, ninety had been delivered to the Wehrmacht. In the strength report of June 1, 1941 there were 81 of these vehicles listed. In January 1942 the last nine of them were to be delivered. The combat action of the Russian campaign, though, raised questions about the effectiveness of the "Flammpanzer II." At the same time, the lack of mobile antitank weapons became more and more evident, so that on December 20, 1941 it was decided to stop the production of the "Flammpanzer II" and use the "Panzerkampfwagen II D/E" chassis for the production of tank destroyers. In the spring of 1942, the 1st Flammpanzer Unit was disbanded on account of overly high material losses. The remaining "Flammpanzer II" were taken to the Altmärkische Kettenfabrik GmbH in Berlin-Spandau and, along with the "Panzer II D/E" tanks sent home for overhauling, rebuilt into self-propelled tank destroyers.

In this respect it must be mentioned that in the spring of 1941 there were also plans to involve the "Panzerkampfwagen II n.A. verstärkt" in flamethrowing-tank production. At a conference at the Daimler-Benz AG on June 19, 1941, this vehicle, among others, was mentioned.

At the same time, leading representatives of the Army Weapons Office expressed their conceptions about rebuilding the "Char de Manoeuvre B 1 bis" (German designation B 2-740 (f)), captured in goodly numbers in France in 1940, into flamethrowing tanks. The flamethrowers were to be prepared by the Koebe firm in Luckenwalde, and the modifications of the upper hull done by Daimler-Benz. The firm of Wegmann was responsible for overseeing the work and instal;ling the flamethrowers. From the late autumn of 1941 to the summer of 1942, sixty of these vehicles were delivered to the troops. In the "Flammpanzer B 2 (f)", the flamethrower was mounted in the bow in place of the 75 mm howitzer. It was driven by a two-stroke gasoline engine and could fire up to 200 plumes of flame 40 to 45 meters. At the rear of the vehicle, the tank for the burning oil was mounted. During the modification, the front area in which the flamethrower was mounted was changed twice. In the first version, the howitzer was merely replaced by the flamethrower and operated by the driver. In the second, the rotating turret of the "Flammpanzer II" was attached to the tank's bow armor and operated by a flamethrower man who sat next to the driver. For his orientation, he had a separate periscope. Of the first and second versions there were 24 units built from November 1941 to August 1942. The last version had a turning flamethrower in a ball mantelet. The flamethrower man sitting next to the driver was given an extra visor with the Driver's Hatch 50 of the "Panzerkampfwagen III and IV."

Men of a repair shop company examine a shot-down Flammpanzer II.

A "Panzer II (Fl)."

On December 20, 1941 it was decided to halt production of the "Flammpanzer II." The klast nine vehicles were to be delivered in January 1942. Despite that, the Army Weapons Office reported that it had already accepted 179 "Panzer II (Fl)", 150 from Alkett in Berlin and 29 from Wegmann in Kassel.

Flammpanzer II on the grounds of the Wegmann AG factory in Kassel after completion. This top view shows clearly the two small flamethrowers on the front track covers and the boxes in which the tanks of burning oil were kept. (WJS)

"Flammenwerfer-Panzerkampfwagen B 2 - 740 (f)" of Panzer Unit 213. This unit was formed in 1941 out of Panzer Replacement Regiment 1 (Erfurt), fought in North Africa until mid-1942, and was then used to defend the Channel Islands of Jersey and Guernsey.

When the attacks of the German Wehrmacht were halted at Stalingrad in July and August 1942, the leadership of the 6th Army requested heavy weapons that were especially suitable for street and building combat. To fight down nests of resistance, they requested the introduction of flamethrowers on armored chassis. The Army Weapons Office then decided that 100 "Panzerkampfwagen III Ausführung M Sd.Kfz. 141/1 (Typ 10/ZW" of those produced by the Mühlenbau und Industrie AG firm at its Amme works in Braunschweig should be turned over, without weapons, to the Wegmann firm in Kassel and rebuilt into "Panzerkampfwagen III (Fl) Sd.Kfz. 141/4." At Wegmanns the vehicles were fitted with spray tubes and 14 mm nozzles in mantle pipes. The supply of burning oil amounted to 1000 liters. With it, 70 to 80 bursts of flame could be fired. The burning-oil pumps were driven by 1.1-liter DKW two-stroke motors. The crew consisted of the flamethrower leader/commander, the flamethrower gunner and the driver.

The "Panzer I" with "Small Flamethrower" installed by the Afrikakorps in Tunisia in 1941. Although there was talk of several such vehicles, this cannot be confirmed to date. It cane be presumed that there was only one such vehicle, which was only used by the troops for a short time. Its utility in desert warfare was questionable. The effect of the flamethrower is based mainly on its high destructive power in the nearby area. In areas like North Africa, in which one's view extended to the horizon, the maximum direct shot ranges of all flat-trajectory guns could be utilized, and the vehicle could have been destroyed at long range by armor-piercing weapons.

In December 1942, Panzer Regiment 24 of the 24th Panzer Division was assigned a flamethrower squadron for use at Stalingrad. In 1943 the ideal strength of this unit included 15 flamethrowing tanks. The Panzer Regiment "GD"

The same vehicle from the front. This Flammpanzer B 2 (f) with tactical number 133 was from the third production series. For the flamethrower gunner, a special periscope in "Fahrersehklappe 50" was installed, and the flamethrower was mounted in a ball mantelet. In all, 36 flame tanks of this type were presumably delivered to the troops.

Demonstration of one of the first "Char B 1" tanks fitted with a flamethrower. In the first version, the French 75 mm howitzer was merely replaced by a flamethrower. The driver also had to operate the flamethrower, and the flamethrower could be aimed only by turning the entire tank. The tank for the burning oil was located in the bow, to the right side of the driver (in later versions it was mounted outside at the rear of the vehicle).

One hundred of the "Flammpanzer III" are believed to have been built. Surprisingly, though, on July 1, 1943 some of them had already been lost at the front. It is still not known why MIAG was to deliver Panzer III without weapons to Wegmann when that firm itself produced Panzer III tanks and turned 373 of them (15 of them repaired) over to the Army Weapons Office in 1942. The picture shows a P III (Fl) during flamethrower crew training. (WJS)

and Regiment 2 of the 16th Panzer Division also were equipped with flamethrowing tanks. In the summer of 1943, still other armored regiments were given Flammpanzer III platoons.

But since the "Flammpanzer III" could not live up to expectations, although the range of the flame was stated officially as 55 to 60 meters, while in practice it never exceeded 35 meters, and since the Panzer III was much too valuable as a battle tank, most flame tanks were eventually rebuilt into normal tanks. A few of them remained with the troops for a fairly long time; in October 1944 there were still eleven in use.

The use of assault guns from ongoing production as "flame tanks" was decided on at the Führer's Headquarters during a discussion in early December 1942. Here a one-time production of ten vehicles was called for. The firms of Wegmann and Koebe were given the rebuilding job. They were to install the same flamethrowers as used in the "Panzerkampfwagen III (Fl)." On January 23, 1943 the first firing tests were carried out with the prototype at Panzer Troop School I in Wünsdorf, and the required flame range of fifty meters was actually exceeded by several meters.

Above and left: The range of the burst of flame was to be between 55 and 60 meters, but in practice it only reached a little over 30 meters. Since the vehicles could not live up to expectations, some of them were rebuilt into battle tank at German repair shops. From July 1942 to August 1943, 37 P III N were armed with 7.5 cm tank guns. It is probable that the vehicles on Type 10/ZW chassis (Version M) were former "Flammpanzer III." (WJS)

After Wegmann had given assurances that the existing faults (among other things, the burning oil had not ignited immediately) would be eliminated, permission for rebuilding was granted. Unlike the original conception, though, vehicles built in past years, that had been sent back from the front for overhauling and were available from the Army Panzer arsenals, were used. In May 1943 nine vehicles were made available from an arsenal, with the last one following a month later. All ten vehicles were sent on June 29, 1943 to Wünsdorf by rail. One vehicle is said to have been burned out during training. It was brought back to the arsenal, repaired, and returned to the Panzer troop school in September 1943. For lack of antitank weapons, these vehicles were rebuilt again into "Assault Guns with 7.5 cm Assault Gun 40 L/48." They were turned over to the arsenal for this purpose in January 1944. In February 1944 seven, in March one and in April 1944 the last two "StuG (Fl)" were reported as rebuilt.

The only flamethrowing vehicle that was regularly supplied to the engineer troops was the "Mittlere Schützenpanzerwagen Sd.Kfz. 251/16." In the Panzer grenadier regiments, according to a war strength document of November 1, 1943, there were six each of these vehicles, also called "Mittlere Flammpanzerwagen", in the 2nd platoon of the staff company and the 4th platoons of the engineer companies. The platoons consisted of one officer (likewise flame leader and radioman), five non-commissioned officers (likewise commanders of the SPW, flame leaders and radiomen), and twelve flamethrower shooters. Their primary weapons consisted of two flamethrowers attached to the sidewalls and manually operated. They could fire forty two-second bursts of flame. The pumping system was likewise powered by the 1.1-liter DKW two-stroke engine, so that a pressure of 15 atmospheres could be created. In addition, every SPW carried one "Flamethrower 41", one "Machine Gun 42", two "Machine Pistol 40" and one "Carbine 98."

The "Sturmgeschütz III (Fl)" was created by rebuilding vehicles that had been sent back to Germany for servicing. It can be assumed from this that all these flamethrowing tanks were originally "Assault Gun III" of the F/8 version. The armored hulls of these vehicles were a delivery of fifty units from the Wegmann firm in Kassel to the Altmärkische Kettenfabrik in Berlin-Tegel. There they were fitted with the assault-gun body. To have machines that were out of action at the front, they were first gathered in equipment depots, sorted out by type and maker, and sent to the appropriate factories. For Wegmann, only the Assault Gun was available, its hulls having been made by that factory itself.

American soldiers examine an abandoned "Flammpanzer 38" in Alsace in January 1945. The vehicle was probably abandoned in the Weissenburg area by Panzer Flame Company 352 because of technical difficulties (engine or gearbox trouble). All flamethrowing tanks were thrown into front-line action in haste, without being broken in properly. Otherwise the vehicle is said to have been extremely satisfactory in technical terms.

In addition, every Panzer grenadier regiment had four three-ton open off-road trucks to carry burning oil and refilling equipment. Three of the trucks were for the SPW and one for the "Fm. W. 41." The drivers of the trucks were also the flamethrower maintenance men. Every man had a rifle or a carbine as his personal weapon.

In preparation for the Ardennes offensive, Hitler personally requested the preparation of at least 20 to 30 flamethrowing tanks. In the period from mid-November to early December 1944, twenty Jagdpanzer 38 (t) "Hetzer" tanks were therefore equipped with flamethrowers (14 mm nozzle) instead of the "7.5 cm Pak 39 L/48" at the Bohemian-Moravian Machine Works in Prague. The nozzle was likewise enclosed, so that the "Flammpanzer 38" could scarcely be told apart from the tank destroyer from outside. In the fighting compartment, the burning-oil container, with a capacity of 700 liters, was installed. The flame jet pressure was created by a centrifugal pump, which attained a flame range of 50 to 60 meters. The bursts of flame were activated by a foot pedal. The maximum duration of fire was 1.5 minutes. All twenty vehicles were assigned to Panzer Flame Companies 352 and 353 and were ultimately lost to technical damage or enemy action.

Another abandoned "Flammpanzer 38." This one has taken a shot in the front end, with the covering of the flamethrower tube being torn away. One last piece of the mantle sheath stands in front of the vehicle. In action, the flamethrowing tanks proved to be effective weapons for attacks against bunkers, fortifications, machine-gun positions, and in street combat.

Above: A Type D SPW (smooth rear end). Below: Drawing of the Type C with flamethrowing mechanism.

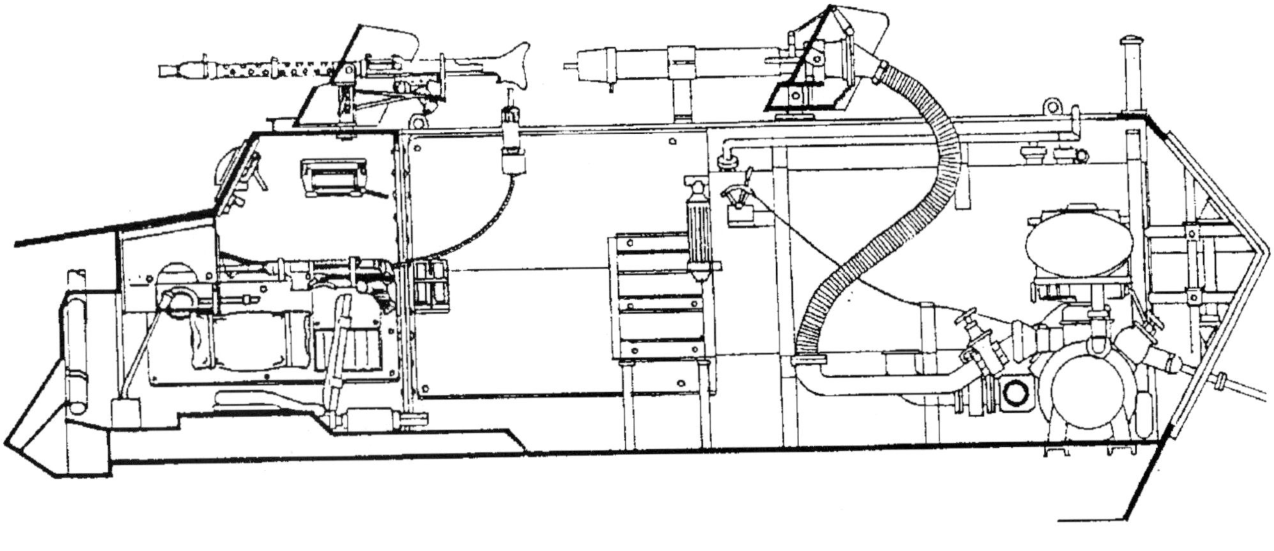

The crew of the "Mittlere Flammpanzerwagen" consisted of three men, one officer or NCO and two gunners. As a rule, though, there were four or even five men in an SPW. This proved to be effective, as the officer or NCO, having three jobs to do simultaneously (commander, driver, radioman), was thoroughly overworked, which sometimes made cooperation with other SPWs impossible. (WJS) The protective clothing seen above was worn only seldom.

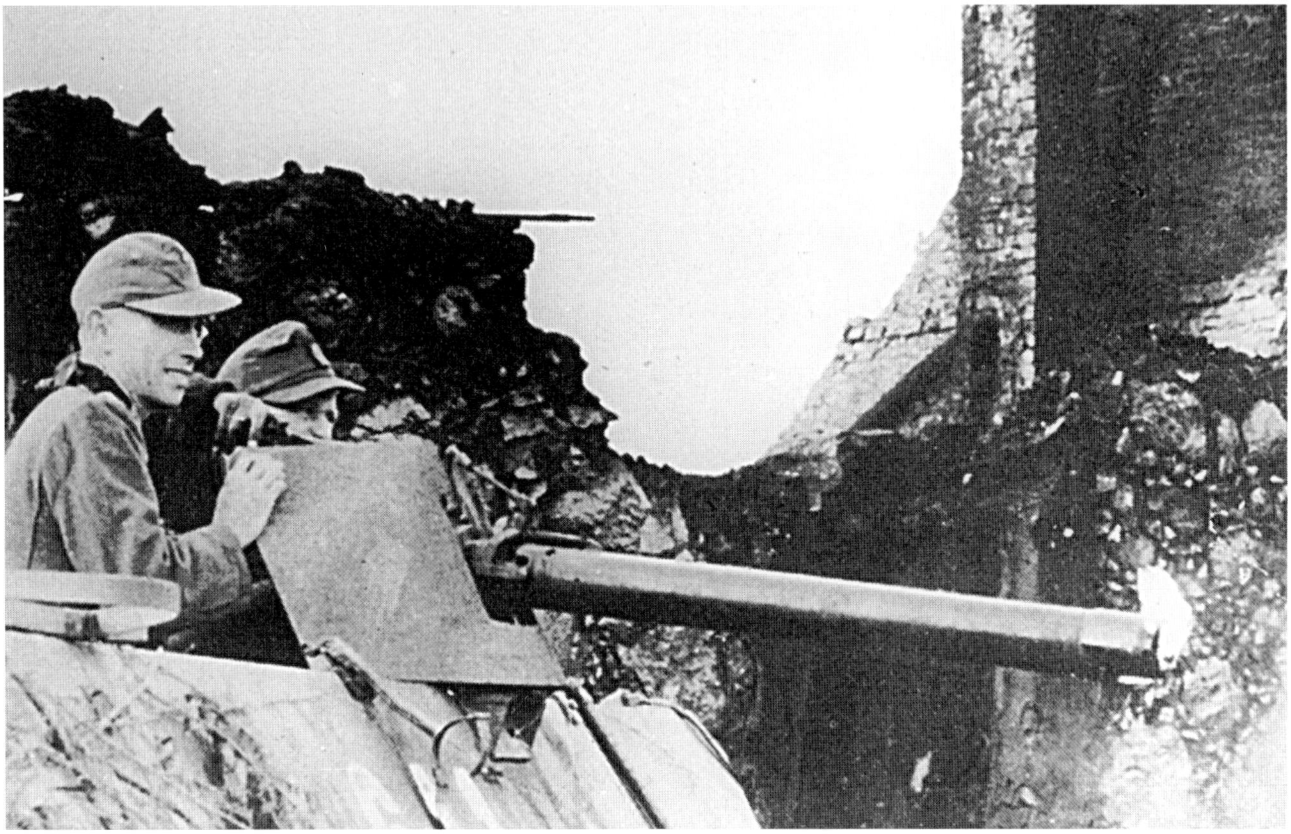

Above: Mittlerer Flammpanzerwagen, Sd. Kfz. 251/16, Type C. (WJS)

A look into the fighting compartment of the "Mittlere Schützenpanzerwagen Sd.Kfz. 251/16." A flamethrower was attached to each of the two sidewalls. Each one could be turned in any direction and had the same shield that was used for the machine gun on the front wall. The burning-oil tank, holding 700 liters, and the gasoline engine that powered the pumps, were located in the rear part of the hull. The vehicle also carried a portable flamethrower, generally the "Fm. W. 41." In addition, every SPW carried two machine pistols and carbines. Each commander carried a pistol as his personal weapon.

Below: The SPW with flamethrowers, built from 1942 to 1944, saw service on all fronts in the war. This SPW seen in Normandy in mid-1944 belonged to the 3rd Company of the SS Engineer Battalion 9 of the 9th SS Panzer Division "Hohenstauffen."

THE 32 cm WURFKÖRPER FLAMM

A flamethrower of a special kind was the 32 cm Wurfkörper Flamm. With a weight of 79.2 kg, it could carry fifty liters of burning oil from 750 to 2200 meters. After impact, the burning oil was sprayed over some 200 square meters. The effect was even heightened by the combined use of explosive shells.

This missile was fired either from the 28/32 cm Foglauncher 41 or right out of its packing case, which was made of either wood or steel. To do this, the packing cases (which held four missiles) were attached to the "Heavy Launcher 40 or 41." They were ignited electrically by a "Glow Ignition Apparatus and Glow Igniter 40 with Delay." In order to fire these missiles from armored vehicles as well, the firm of I. Gast KG in Berlin-Lichtenberg built the "Heavy Launching Frame 40" for 1582 Reichsmark apiece. The individual packing cases were attached to this and the missiles fired from them. Triggering could be done by a sixfold ignition machine or by the Push-Button Igniter 42. The launcher brigades directly subordinated to the O.K.H. were equipped with these weapons.

32 cm missiles in their wooden packing case on the "Heavy Launcher 40", likewise made of wood.

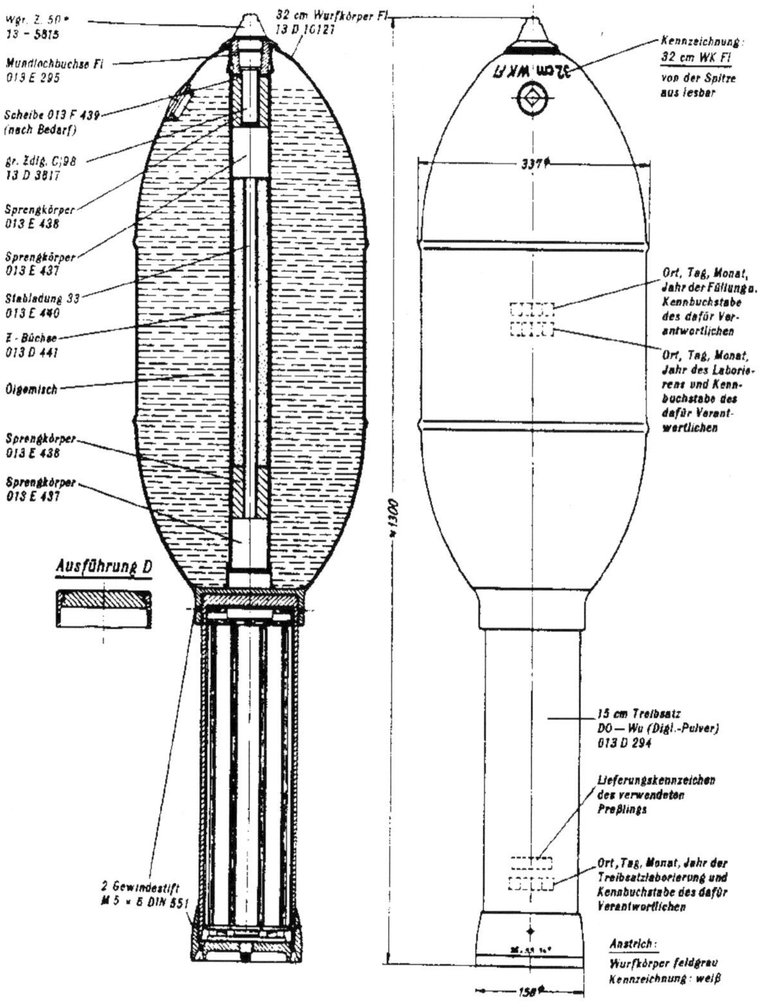

Right: The "Heavy Launcher 41" with four 32 cm missiles in wooden packing cases. This was likewise built by the firm of I. Gast KG. The price per piece was 298.70 RM, the steel packing case cost 45.50 RM and the missile without its contents cost 33.12 RM. The firm could produce 25 "sWG 41" per day. The production of 100 packing cases took about eight days, and that of 100 missiles took about two months. A wooden packing case weighed 30 kg, one of steel 10 kg less, and the launcher weighed 110 kg.

Below: The "Heavy Launcher 40" was built especially for the "Mittlere Schützenpanzerwagen Sd. Kfz. 251/1." The vehicle was nicknamed "Stuka zu Fuß" by the soldiers. Some described it, on account of the noticeable exhaust fumes, as the "Howling Cow." The "sWuR 40" was also built on the French Hotchkiss 38H-735 (f) and UE-630 (f) armored vehicle chassis.

In conclusion, it should be noted that all captured flamethrowing vehicles were evaluated as to their capacity for reuse and put into service individually, particularly the Russian flamethrowers on T 26, T 34 and KW-1 chassis. But there were also individual rebuildings by the troops. For example, several "Light Armored Scout Cars, Sd. Kfz. 222" were equipped with a flamethrower (as seen at left).

The Spielberger German Armor & Military Vehicles Series

Four volumes in the classic series by reknowned German panzer historian Walter Spielberger are now available in ne English editions. Known for his emphasis on detail, Spielberger chronicles each production variation and later modifications. Line drawings by Hilary Doyle complement the discussion of each model type.

Size: 8 1/2" x 11" 288 pages hard cover
over 460 photographs
ISBN: 0-88740-397-2 $39.95

Size: 8 1/2" x 11" 256 pages hard cover
over 240 photographs
ISBN: 0-88740-398-0 $39.95

Size: 8 1/2" x 11" 168 pages hard cover
over 200 photographs
ISBN: 0-88740-448-0 $29.95

Size: 8 1/2" x 11" 168 pages hard cover
over 200 photographs
ISBN: 0-88740-515-0 $29.95